FOLK SONGS

FOR OCARINA

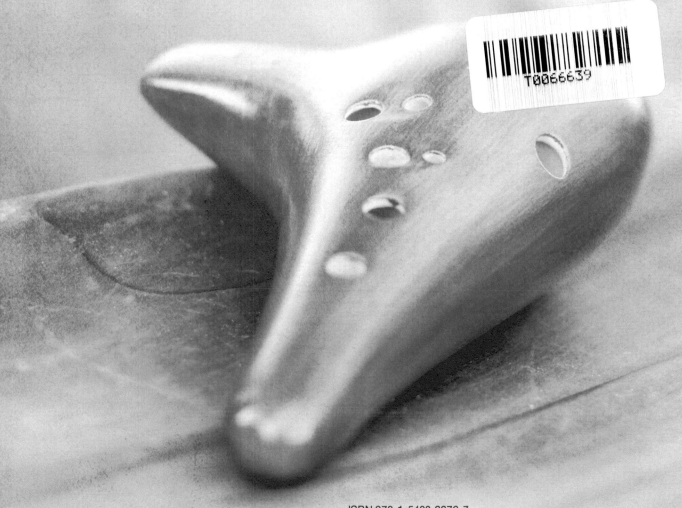

T0066639

ISBN 978-1-5400-2676-7

HAL•LEONARD®

Copyright © 2018 by HAL LEONARD LLC
International Copyright Secured All Rights Reserved

For all works contained herein:
Unauthorized copying, arranging, adapting, recording, Internet posting, public performance,
or other distribution of the music in this publication is an infringement of copyright.
Infringers are liable under the law.

Visit Hal Leonard Online at
www.halleonard.com

Contact Us:
Hal Leonard
7777 West Bluemound Road
Milwaukee, WI 53213
Email: info@halleonard.com

In Europe contact:
Hal Leonard Europe Limited
Distribution Centre, Newmarket Road
Bury St Edmunds, Suffolk, IP33 3YB
Email: info@halleonardeurope.com

In Australia contact:
Hal Leonard Australia Pty. Ltd.
4 Lentara Court
Cheltenham, Victoria, 3192 Australia
Email: info@halleonard.com.au

CONTENTS

4

ALL THE PRETTY LITTLE HORSES

Copyright © 2018 by HAL LEONARD LLC
International Copyright Secured   All Rights Reserved

Southeastern American Lullaby

Relaxed

Hush - you - bye, don't you cry, go to sleep - y, lit - tle ba - by.

When you wake, you shall have all the pret - ty lit - tle hors - es.

(small note optional)

Blacks and bays, dap - ples and greys, coach and six - a - lit - tle hors - es.

Hush - you - bye, don't you cry, go to sleep - y, lit - tle ba - by.

ALOUETTE

Copyright © 2018 by HAL LEONARD LLC
International Copyright Secured   All Rights Reserved

Traditional

Moderately

A - lou - et - te, gen - tille A - lou - et - te, A - lou - et - te, je te plu - me - rai.

Je te plu - me - rai la tête, Je te plu - me - rai la tête, et la tête, et la tête, O!

A - lou - et - te, gen - tille A - lou - et - te, A - lou - et - te, je te plu - me - rai.

AMAZING GRACE

Copyright © 2018 by HAL LEONARD LLC
International Copyright Secured   All Rights Reserved

Words by JOHN NEWTON
Traditional American Melody

ANNIE LAURIE

Copyright © 2018 by HAL LEONARD LLC
International Copyright Secured   All Rights Reserved

Words by WILLIAM DOUGLAS
Music by LADY JOHN SCOTT

AULD LANG SYNE

Copyright © 2018 by HAL LEONARD LLC
International Copyright Secured   All Rights Reserved

Words by ROBERT BURNS
Traditional Scottish Melody

AURA LEE

Copyright © 2018 by HAL LEONARD LLC
International Copyright Secured   All Rights Reserved

Words by W.W. FOSDICK
Music by GEORGE R. POULTON

THE BANANA BOAT SONG

Copyright © 2018 by HAL LEONARD LLC
International Copyright Secured   All Rights Reserved

Jamaican Work Song

Day oh! Day — oh! Day da light — an' me wan' go home.

Come Mis-ter Tall-y-man, come tall-y me ba-na-na. Day da light — an' me

wan' go home. Six hand, sev-en hand, eight hand bunch! Six hand, sev-en hand
We load ba-na-nas till the ear-ly light. Sleep all day and

eight hand bunch!} Day da light — an' me wan' go home. Day oh!
work all night. }

Day — oh! Day da light — an' me wan' go home.

FRÈRE JACQUES
(Are You Sleeping?)

Copyright © 2018 by HAL LEONARD LLC
International Copyright Secured   All Rights Reserved

Traditional

Are you sleep-ing? Are you sleep-ing? Broth-er
Frè-re Jac-ques, Frè-re Jac-ques, Dor-mez-

John, Broth-er John, morn-ing bells are ring-ing,
vous? Dor-mez-vous? son-nez les ma-ti-nes,

morn-ing bells are ring-ing: Ding, dang, dong! Ding, dang, dong!
son-nez les ma-ti-nes: Ding, din, don! Ding, din, don!

THE BLUE BELLS OF SCOTLAND

Copyright © 2018 by HAL LEONARD LLC
International Copyright Secured   All Rights Reserved

Words and Music attributed to
MRS. JORDON

Moderately

Oh where, tell me where is your __ High - land lad - die gone? Oh

where, tell me where is your __ High - land lad - die gone? He's

gone wi' stream - ing ban - ners where __ no - ble deeds are done, and it's

oh, in my heart I _____ wish him safe at home.

DANNY BOY

Copyright © 2018 by HAL LEONARD LLC
International Copyright Secured   All Rights Reserved

Words by FREDERICK EDWARD WEATHERLY
Traditional Irish Folk Melody

Slowly
(small notes optional)

Oh, Dan - ny Boy, the pipes, the pipes are call - ing _____ from glen to

glen and down the moun - tain side. _____ The sum - mer's gone and all the ros - es

fall - ing, 'tis you, 'tis you must go and I must bide. But come ye

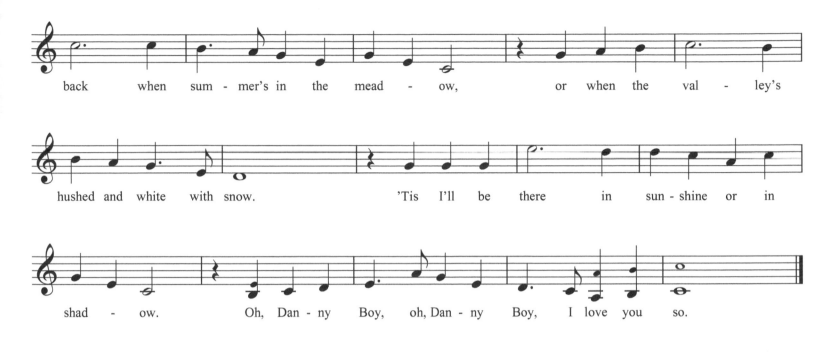

back when sum - mer's in the mead - ow, or when the val - ley's

hushed and white with snow. 'Tis I'll be there in sun - shine or in

shad - ow. Oh, Dan - ny Boy, oh, Dan - ny Boy, I love you so.

FOLLOW THE DRINKIN' GOURD

Copyright © 2018 by HAL LEONARD LLC
International Copyright Secured   All Rights Reserved

African-American Spiritual

Rhythmically

When the sun comes back and the first quail calls, ___ fol - low the drink - in' gourd, for the

old man's wait - in' for to car - ry you to free-dom. Fol - low the drink - in' gourd.

Fol - low the drink - in' gourd. _ Fol - low the drink - in' gourd, for the

old man is a - wait - in' for to car - ry you to free-dom. Fol - low the drink - in' gourd.

HAVA NAGILA
(Let's Be Happy)

Copyright © 2018 by HAL LEONARD LLC
International Copyright Secured   All Rights Reserved

Lyrics by MOSHE NATHANSON
Music by ABRAHAM Z. IDELSOHN

With spirit

Ha - va _____ na - gi - la Ha - va _____ na - gi - la Ha - va _____

_____ na - gi - la v' - nis m' - cha.   Ha - va _____ na - gi - la

Ha - va _____ na - gi - la Ha - va _____ na - gi - la v' - nis m' -

cha.   Ha - va n' - ra - n' na   Ha - va n' - rah - n' na

Ha - va n' - ra - n' na v' - nis m' - cha.   Ha - va n' -

ra - n' na   Ha - va n' - ra - n' na   Ha - va n' - rah - n' na

v' - nis m' - cha.   U - ru,   U - ru a - chim,

U - ru a - chim B' - lev sa - mey - ach,   U - ru a - chim B' - lev sa - mey - ach,

U - ru a - chim B' - lev sa - mey - ach.   U - ru a - chim B' - lev sa - mey - ach,

U - ru a - chim,   U - ru a - chim B'lev sa - mey - ach.

JOSHUA
(Fit the Battle of Jericho)

Copyright © 2018 by HAL LEONARD LLC
International Copyright Secured   All Rights Reserved

African-American Spiritual

12

GREENSLEEVES

Copyright © 2018 by HAL LEONARD LLC
International Copyright Secured   All Rights Reserved

Sixteenth Century Traditional English

Slowly

A - las, my love, __ you do me wrong __ to cast me off __ dis - cour - teous - ly. And

I have loved __ you oh, so long __ de - light - ing in __ your com - pa - ny.

Green - sleeves __ was all my joy. _____ Green - sleeves __ was my de - light.

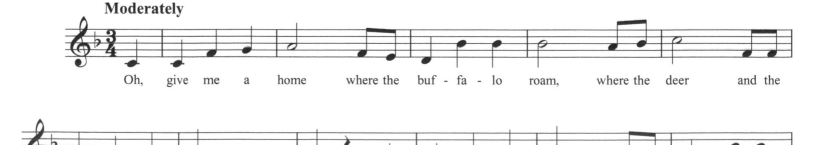

Green - sleeves was my heart of gold, __ and who but my la - dy Green - sleeves.

HOME ON THE RANGE

Copyright © 2018 by HAL LEONARD LLC
International Copyright Secured   All Rights Reserved

Lyrics by DR. BREWSTER HIGLEY
Music by DAN KELLY

Moderately

Oh, give me a home where the buf - fa - lo roam, where the deer and the

an - te - lope play, _____ where sel - dom is heard a dis - cour - ag - ing

word, and the skies are not cloud-y all day. _____

Home, home on the range, _____ where the deer and the

an-te-lope play; _____ where sel-dom is heard a dis-

cour-ag-ing word, and the skies are not cloud-y all day.

HUSH, LITTLE BABY

Copyright © 2018 by HAL LEONARD LLC
International Copyright Secured All Rights Reserved

Carolina Folk Lullaby

Moderately

Hush, lit-tle ba-by, don't say a word, Pa-pa's gon-na buy you a mock-ing-bird. And
If that __ dia-mond ring is __ brass, Pa-pa's gon-na buy you a look-ing glass. And
If that __ jump-ing jack won't hop, Pa-pa's gon-na buy you a lol-li-pop.
If that __ lol-li-pop is eat-en up, Pa-pa's gon-na buy you a real live pup.

if that mock-ing-bird don't sing, Pa-pa's gon-na buy you a dia-mond ring.
if that look-ing glass should crack, Pa-pa's gon-na buy you a jump-ing jack.
When that lol-li-pop is done, Pa-pa's gon-na buy you an-oth-er one.
If that pup-py dog won't bark, Pa-pa's gon-na buy you a mead-ow-lark.

KUMBAYA

Copyright © 2018 by HAL LEONARD LLC
International Copyright Secured   All Rights Reserved

Congo Folksong

Relaxed

Kum - ba - ya, my Lord, Kum - ba - ya. Kum - ba - ya, my Lord, Kum - ba -

ya. Kum - ba - ya, my Lord, Kum - ba - ya. Oh, Lord, __ Kum - ba - ya.

LA CUCARACHA

Copyright © 2018 by HAL LEONARD LLC
International Copyright Secured   All Rights Reserved

Mexican Revolutionary Folksong

Brightly

MY OLD KENTUCKY HOME

Copyright © 2018 by HAL LEONARD LLC
International Copyright Secured   All Rights Reserved

Words and Music by
STEPHEN C. FOSTER

Gently

The sun shines bright in the old Ken-tuck-y home; 'tis sum-mer, the folks there are gay. The corn top's ripe and the mead-ow's in the bloom, while the birds make mu-sic all the day. The young folks roll on the lit-tle cab-in floor, all mer-ry, all hap-py and bright. By'n by hard times comes a-knock-ing at the door; then my old Ken-tuck-y home, good night! Weep no more, my la-dy, oh, weep no more to-day! We will sing one song for the old Ken-tuck-y home, for the old Ken-tuck-y home far a-way.

LITTLE BROWN JUG

Copyright © 2018 by HAL LEONARD LLC
International Copyright Secured   All Rights Reserved

Words and Music by
JOSEPH E. WINNER

Brightly

My wife and I, ___ we live a - lone ___ in a lit - tle log hut we

call our own. ___ She loves gin ___ and I love rum, ___ to - geth - er we have

lots of fun. ___ Ha ha ha, you and me, lit - tle brown jug, how

I love thee. Ha ha ha, you and me, lit - tle brown jug, how I love thee.

LOCH LOMOND

Copyright © 2018 by HAL LEONARD LLC
International Copyright Secured All Rights Reserved

Scottish Folk Song

Moderately slow

By ___ yon bon - nie banks and by yon bon - nie braes, where the sun shines bright on Loch

Lo - mond, where me and my true love were ev - er wont to be on the

bon - nie, bon - nie banks of Loch Lo - mond. Oh, you'll take the high road and

I'll take the low road and I'll be in Scot - land be - fore you. But me and my true love will

nev - er meet a - gain on the bon - nie, bon - nie banks of Loch Lo - mond.

MY BONNIE LIES OVER THE OCEAN

Copyright © 2018 by HAL LEONARD LLC
International Copyright Secured   All Rights Reserved

Traditional

Quickly

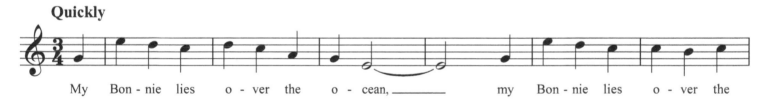

My Bon - nie lies o - ver the o - cean, _____ my Bon - nie lies o - ver the

sea. _____ My Bon - nie lies o - ver the o - cean, _____ oh

bring back my Bon - nie to me. _____ Bring back, bring

back, bring back my Bon - nie to me, to me. Bring

back, bring back, oh bring back my Bon - nie to me. _____

MY WILD IRISH ROSE

Copyright © 2018 by HAL LEONARD LLC
International Copyright Secured   All Rights Reserved

Words and Music by
CHAUNCEY OLCOTT

Slowly

My wild I - rish rose, the sweet-est flow'r that grows, you may search ev -'ry - where but none can com - pare with my wild I - rish rose. My wild I - rish rose, the dear-est flow'r that grows, and some day, for my sake, she may let me take the bloom from my wild I - rish rose.

OH! SUSANNA

Copyright © 2018 by HAL LEONARD LLC
International Copyright Secured All Rights Reserved

Words and Music by
STEPHEN C. FOSTER

Lively

I come from Al - a - bam - a with a ban - jo on my knee. I'm goin' to Lou' - si - an - a, my Su - san - na for to

see. It __ rained all night the day I left, the weath-er it was

dry. The __ sun so hot I froze to death. Su-san-na, don't you

cry. Oh! Su - san - na, oh, don't you cry for

me, for I come from Al - a - bam - a with a ban-jo on my knee.

OLD DAN TUCKER

Copyright © 2018 by HAL LEONARD LLC
International Copyright Secured   All Rights Reserved

Traditional

Lively

Went to town the oth - er night, to hear a noise and see a fight.

All the peo-ple were run-ning a-round say-ing old Dan Tuck-er's come to town.

Get out the way, old Dan Tuck - er, you're too late to come for sup-per.

Sup-per's o-ver and din-ner's cook-ing and old Dan Tuck-er just stand-ing there look-ing.

20

SAKURA
(Cherry Blossoms)

Copyright © 2018 by HAL LEONARD LLC
International Copyright Secured   All Rights Reserved

Traditional Japanese Folksong

Gently

Sa - ku - ra! Sa - ku - ra! Ya yo - i no so ra — wa
Sa - ku - ra! Sa - ku - ra! Cher - ry blos - soms fill the — air,

Mi wa - ta - su ka - gi - ri Ka - su - mi ka ku - mo — ka, Ni o - i - zo
smell their fra - grance ev - 'ry - where. Win - ter - time is fi - n'lly — past, now the spring is

i - zu - ru. I - za - ya! I - za - ya! Mi — ni — yu - kan.
here at — last. Come with me! Come with me! Let us feel the sun - shine fair.

SCARBOROUGH FAIR

Copyright © 2018 by HAL LEONARD LLC
International Copyright Secured   All Rights Reserved

Traditional English

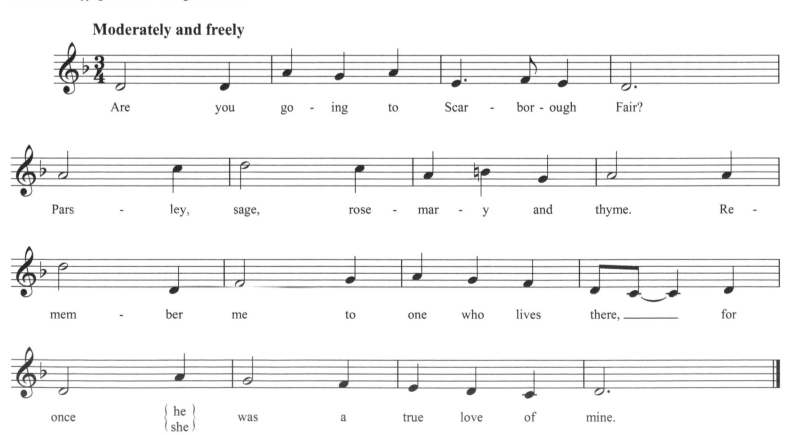

Moderately and freely

Are you go - ing to Scar - bor - ough Fair?

Pars - ley, sage, rose - mar - y and thyme. Re -

mem - ber me to one who lives there, _____ for

once { he } { she } was a true love of mine.

SHENANDOAH

Copyright © 2018 by HAL LEONARD LLC
International Copyright Secured   All Rights Reserved

American Folk Song

Moderately, with feeling

Oh, Shen - an - doah, __ I long to hear you, a - way, __ you roll - ing riv - er. Oh, Shen - an - doah, __ I love to hear you, a - way, __ I'm bound a - way, 'cross the wide __ Mis - sou - ri.

SIMPLE GIFTS

Copyright © 2018 by HAL LEONARD LLC
International Copyright Secured   All Rights Reserved

Traditional Shaker Hymn

Warmly

'Tis the gift to be sim - ple, 'tis the gift to be free, 'tis the gift to come down where we ought to be, and when we find our - selves in the place just right, 'twill be in the val - ley of love and de - light. When true sim - plic - i - ty is gained, to bow and to bend we __ shan't be a - shamed. To turn, turn will be our de - light till by turn - ing and turn - ing we come 'round right.

SOMETIMES I FEEL LIKE A MOTHERLESS CHILD

Copyright © 2018 by HAL LEONARD LLC
International Copyright Secured   All Rights Reserved

African-American Spiritual

Some-times I feel like a moth-er-less child, some-times I feel like a

moth-er-less child, some-times I feel like a moth-er-less child, A

long way — from home, ———— a long way — from home. ———— A

long way — from home, ———— a long way — from home.

SKIP TO MY LOU

Copyright © 2018 by HAL LEONARD LLC
International Copyright Secured   All Rights Reserved

Traditional

Lou, lou, skip to my lou, lou, lou, skip to my lou,

lou, lou, skip to my lou, skip to my lou, my dar - ling.

Lost my part - ner, what - 'll I do? Lost my part - ner, what - 'll I do?

Lost my part - ner, what - 'll I do? Skip to my lou, my dar - ling.

Lou, lou, skip to my lou, lou, lou, skip to my lou,

lou, lou, skip to my lou, skip to my lou, my dar - ling.

THERE IS A BALM IN GILEAD

Copyright © 2018 by HAL LEONARD LLC
International Copyright Secured   All Rights Reserved

African-American Spiritual

Soulfully

There _ is a balm in Gil - e - ad to make the wound - ed

whole, _____ there _ is a balm in Gil - e - ad to

heal the sin - sick soul. Some - times I feel dis - cour - aged and

think my work's in vain, but then the Ho - ly Spir - it re -

vives my soul a - gain. _____ There _ is a balm in

Gil - e - ad to make the wound - ed whole, _____ there _ is a

balm in Gil - e - ad to heal the sin - sick soul.

SWING LOW, SWEET CHARIOT

Copyright © 2018 by HAL LEONARD LLC
International Copyright Secured   All Rights Reserved

Traditional Spiritual

Moderately

Swing low, sweet char - i - ot, ___ com-ing for to car-ry me home.

Swing _ low, sweet char - i - ot, ___ com-ing for to car-ry me home.   { I / If

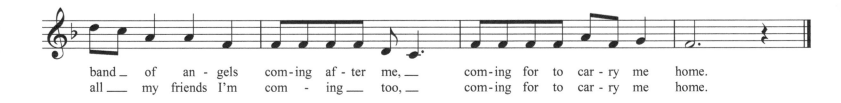

looked o - ver Jor - dan and what did I see? ___ Com-ing for to car-ry me home,   a
you _ get there be - fore _ I do, ___ com-ing for to car-ry me home,   tell

band _ of an - gels com-ing af - ter me, ___ com-ing for to car-ry me home.
all ___ my friends I'm com - ing _ too, ___ com-ing for to car-ry me home.

TWINKLE, TWINKLE LITTLE STAR

Copyright © 2018 by HAL LEONARD LLC
International Copyright Secured   All Rights Reserved

Traditional

Gently

Twin - kle, twin - kle, lit - tle star, how I won - der

what you are! Up a - bove the world so high,

like a dia - mond in the sky. Twin - kle, twin - kle,

lit - tle star, how I won - der what you are!

VOLGA BOATMAN SONG

Copyright © 2018 by HAL LEONARD LLC
International Copyright Secured   All Rights Reserved

Russian Folk Song

Slowly

Ei, __ oo - kyem! Ei, __ oo - kyem! Yeh - sho ra - zik, yeh - sho raz!

Ei, __ oo - kyem! Ei, __ oo - kyem! Yeh - sho ra - zik, yeh - sho __ raz!

Ra - zo - vyom __ mi __ ber - yo - zoh, Ra - zo - vyom __ mi __

ber - yo - zoh, Ai da da ai da, ai da da ai da, ra - zo - vyom __ mi

koo - dria - voh. Ra - zo - vyom __ mi koo - dria - voh.

WERE YOU THERE?

Copyright © 2018 by HAL LEONARD LLC
International Copyright Secured   All Rights Reserved

Traditional Spiritual

Were you there when they cru - ci - fied my Lord? _____ Were you

there when they cru - ci - fied my Lord? _____ Oh, _____

some - times it caus - es me to trem - ble, trem - ble, trem - ble. Were you

there when they cru - ci - fied my Lord? _____

WHEN JOHNNY COMES MARCHING HOME

Copyright © 2018 by HAL LEONARD LLC
International Copyright Secured   All Rights Reserved

Words and Music by
PATRICK SARSFIELD GILMORE

When John - ny comes march - ing home a - gain, hur - rah! _____ Hur - rah! _____ We'll

give him a heart - y wel - come then, hur - rah! _____ Hur - rah! _____ Oh, the

men will cheer and the boys will shout. The la - dies they _ will all turn out. And we'll

all feel gay when John - ny comes march - ing home.

WHEN THE SAINTS GO MARCHING IN

Copyright © 2018 by HAL LEONARD LLC
International Copyright Secured   All Rights Reserved

Words by KATHERINE E. PURVIS
Music by JAMES M. BLACK

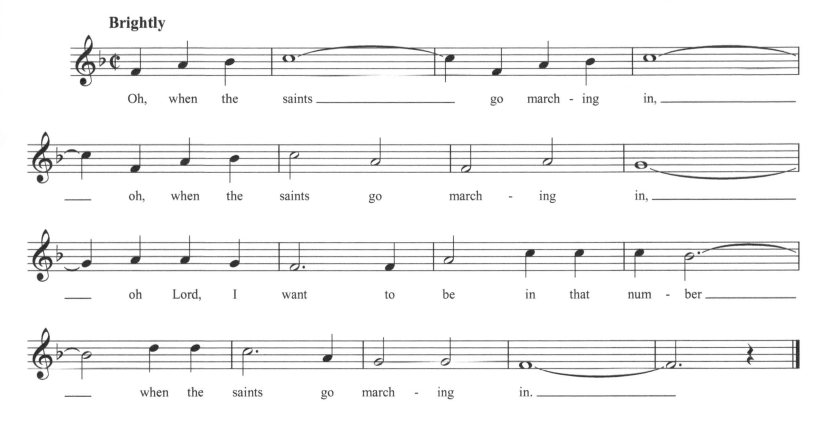

YANKEE DOODLE

Copyright © 2018 by HAL LEONARD LLC
International Copyright Secured   All Rights Reserved

Traditional

THIS LITTLE LIGHT OF MINE

Copyright © 2018 by HAL LEONARD LLC
International Copyright Secured   All Rights Reserved

African-American Spiritual

Moderately

This lit-tle light of mine, __ I'm gon-na let it shine, __

this lit-tle light of mine, __ I'm gon-na let it shine. __

This lit-tle light of mine, __ I'm gon-na let it shine __ ev-'ry

To Coda

day, ev-'ry day, ev-'ry day, ev-'ry day __ gon-na let my lit-tle light

shine. __ On Mon-day He gave me the gift of love, on

Tues-day peace came from a-bove, on Wednes-day told me to have more faith, on

Thurs-day gave me a lit-tle more grace. On Fri-day told me to watch and pray, on

Sat-ur-day told me just what to say, on Sun-day gave me the pow-er di-vine, just to

D.C. al Coda

let my lit-tle light shine.

CODA

shine. __

THE YELLOW ROSE OF TEXAS

Copyright © 2018 by HAL LEONARD LLC
International Copyright Secured All Rights Reserved

Words and Music by
J.K., 1858

Moderately

There's a yel - low rose in Tex - as that __ I am goin' to see. No

oth - er fel - low loves her, no - bod - y, on - ly me. She

cried so when I left her, it __ like to broke my heart. And

if I ev - er find her, we nev - er - more will part. She's the

sweet - est rose of col - or this fel - low ev - er knew. Her

eyes are bright as dia - monds, they spar - kle like the dew. You may

talk a - bout your dear - est May, and sing of Ro - sa Lee. But the

Yel - low Rose of Tex - as beats the belles of Ten - nes - see.

12-Hole Ocarina Fingering Chart

MORE GREAT OCARINA PUBLICATIONS

Christmas Carols for Ocarina

Arranged for 10, 11 & 12-Hole Ocarinas
30 favorite carols of the holiday season: Angels We Have Heard on High • Away in a Manger • Coventry Carol • Deck the Hall • God Rest Ye Merry, Gentlemen • It Came upon the Midnight Clear • Jingle Bells • Joy to the World • O Come, All Ye Faithful • O Holy Night • Silent Night • Up on the Housetop • We Wish You a Merry Christmas • and more.

00277990 ....$9.99

Christmas Favorites for Ocarina

Arranged for 10, 11 & 12-Hole Ocarinas
Play 23 holiday classics in arrangements tailored to this unique wind instrument: Blue Christmas • Christmas Time Is Here • Do You Hear What I Hear • Frosty the Snow Man • Have Yourself a Merry Little Christmas • The Little Drummer Boy • The Most Wonderful Time of the Year • Rockin' Around the Christmas Tree • Silver Bells • White Christmas • Winter Wonderland • and more.

00277989 ....$9.99

Disney Songs for Ocarina

Arranged for 10, 11 & 12-Hole Ocarinas
30 Disney favorites, including: Be Our Guest • Can You Feel the Love Tonight • Colors of the Wind • Do You Want to Build a Snowman? • Evermore • He's a Pirate • How Far I'll Go • Kiss the Girl • Lava • Mickey Mouse March • Seize the Day • That's How You Know • When You Wish Upon a Star • A Whole New World • You've Got a Friend in Me • Zip-A-Dee-Doo-Dah • and more..

00275998 .... $10.99

Easy Pop Melodies for Ocarina

Arranged for 10, 11 & 12-Hole Ocarinas
30 popular hits: Believer • City of Stars • Every Breath You Take • Hallelujah • Happy • I'm Yours • The Lion Sleeps Tonight • My Heart Will Go on (Love Theme from *Titanic*) • Perfect • Rolling in the Deep • Shake It Off • Some Nights • The Sound of Silence • Stay with Me • Sweet Caroline • Uptown Girl • What a Wonderful World • Yesterday • You've Got a Friend • and more.

00275999 .... $9.99

Folk Songs for Ocarina

Arranged for 10, 11 & 12-Hole Ocarinass
41 well-known songs: Alouette • Aura Lee • The Banana Boat Song • Follow the Drinkin' Gourd • Frere Jacques (Are You Sleeping?) • Hava Nagila (Let's Be Happy) • Home on the Range • Hush, Little Baby • Joshua (Fit the Battle of Jericho) • Kumbaya • La Cucaracha • Loch Lomond • My Bonnie Lies over the Ocean • My Old Kentucky Home • My Wild Irish Rose • Oh! Susanna • Scarborough Fair • Shenandoah • Swing Low, Sweet Chariot • This Little Light of Mine • Twinkle, Twinkle Little Star • Volga Boatman Song • When Johnny Comes Marching Home • The Yellow Rose of Texas • and more.

00276000...$9.99

Hal Leonard Ocarina Method
by Cris Gale

The Hal Leonard Ocarina Method is a comprehensive, easy-to-use beginner's guide, designed for anyone just learning to play the ocarina. Inside you'll find loads of techniques, tips and fun songs to learn and play. The accompanying online video, featuring author Cris Gale, provides further instruction as well as demonstrations of the music in the book. Topics covered include: a history of the ocarina • types of ocarinas • breathing and articulation • note names and key signatures • meter signatures and rhythmic notation • fingering charts • many classic folksongs • and more.

00146676 Book/Online Video.....................................$14.99

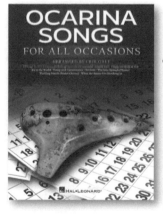

Ocarina Songs for All Occasions

Arranged for 10, 11 & 12-Hole Ocarinas
arr. Cris Gale
30 songs for every season: America, the Beautiful • Auld Lang Syne • Danny Boy • Hail to the Chief • Happy Birthday to You • Joy to the World • The Old Rugged Cross • Pomp and Circumstance • Sevivon • The Star-Spangled Banner • Wedding March (Bridal Chorus) • When the Saints Go Marching In • and more.

00323196...$9.99

HAL•LEONARD®
WWW.HALLEONARD.COM

Prices, contents, and availability subject to change without notice.
Disney characters and artwork TM & © 2021 Disney